To Aunt Zita,
the one
who scatters
sunflowers.

S.F.

EVERYDAY GIFTS

Written and Illustrated by Susan Squellati Florence
The C.R. Gibson Company, Norwalk, CT 06856

*E*veryday gifts line the path of our lives. Like sunflowers blooming along the highway, they often go unnoticed as we speed by. Butterflies, bees, and birds receive nectar from the sunflower and carry pollen from flower to flower. We too are sharing our gifts with each other.

It is in our everyday relationships, that we challenge and define ourselves. With those we love, with those we barely know, and with ourselves we grow and learn about who we are. It is in ordinary moments that we experience the sacred part of life. By this giving and receiving of ourselves we become everyday gifts to each other.

S.F.

Table of Contents

1. Gifts of Parents and Children   P.10

2. Gifts of Your Self   P.26

3. Gifts of Loving   P.38

4. Gifts of Friends   P.48

5. Gifts of Sacred Moments   P.58

*W*hen *our first child was born we received a card from an older man we hardly knew. Nicholas lived alone in the Northern California town of Half Moon Bay. His wife and only son had both died. Besides being a good neighbor, Nicholas had become the adopted grandfather of our friends, Tommy and Dixie. When they moved to the small town in Southern California where we live, Nicholas would visit them. Like a grandfather, he was always fixing things and helping our friends with their home. Years later, when Brent was born, Nicholas sent us a card that I still cherish. On the bottom he wrote something that I will never forget. "By now," he said, "I guess you know what real love is. And in time you will learn to understand and to forgive."*

Nicholas knew what life had given us with the birth of our son...real love. And I knew even before our daughter Emily was born that this incredible gift would enter our lives again.

When my father died, I again felt the power of real love and understood that time does not matter to the loving heart. Comfort surrounded me. One expression of sympathy I will always remember came from my friend Diana, who had lost her mother many years ago. All I knew about her mother was that she had died of breast cancer. Soon after I returned home from my father's funeral there was a knock at the door. Diana stood there holding a most beautiful bouquet of flowers. As she handed me this bouquet, she put her hand over her heart and said two words, "My mother."

We didn't talk. We shared the power of the love that lives on in the hearts of all who have lost a parent. This love is forever.   S.F.

Gifts of Parents
and Children

Babies Take Us On a Special Journey

Babies take us on a special journey
into the land of love.
They bring us to a place that we never knew existed...
but was always there inside...
just waiting for a child to open the door.

This is the place where loving begins...
and we find that by giving we become full.

Babies bring us back to our own small beginnings.
Knowing we were once so small and dependent,
we once again meet the child in ourselves.

We see our parents in a new way,
and know how much we mean to them.

Babies bring us to a new awareness.
Many things we took for granted
become small wonders:
the wonder of growing, of moving, of touching.

Babies teach us many things:
that order is not as stimulating as messes,
that schedules are flexible,
that there is no such thing as a full night's sleep.

Most of all, we learn that time
(which is so precious to us)
means nothing to our baby.

We touch, and hug, and hold, and rock gently,
as time stands still.

And we know without a single word,
the love that exists between us.

The world changes as we follow our little one.
We pause to watch a bug crawl by, a butterfly soar,
and a frog leap.

We find that puddles are for stepping in, not over,
that lawns feel good under bare feet,
and worms are fun to hold!

There will be times when you wonder
why you ever took this journey,
where too much is expected of you,
where the tug and pull and demands on your time
leave you tired and frustrated.

This is the time to stop.
To listen to yourself,
to fill your own needs,
to take a break,
to ask for help.

Your happiness is as important to baby as
baby's happiness is to you.

Through the years your baby will grow,
and as mother or father all the care and nurturing
and time you have given,
will not be needed.

But what your child will always need
is the love you've shared.
This endless circle of love returned
will always nurture your child.

Babies take us on a special journey,
to the land of love within our hearts.

October

I am outside barefoot
playing football
with my son
in the dark.

It is hard to catch the ball
and my feet are soaking wet
from the dew of the night
on the lawn.

And I wonder
what I will be doing
at night
when he is grown and gone.

Will I be out
on the wet lawn
in the dark
playing ball?

And I know
that I have a responsibility
to the child within myself.

It pushes me
plays with me
laughs with me
jumps with me...
I need to keep this part of me.

Or I will truly
be left inside
old, comfortable and bored.

Only One Gift To Give Our Children

Babies give birth
to love
in all our hearts.

As soon as they are born,
they teach us
the language of the heart.

They hold our hands
and gently lead us
into places of deep feelings
and the miracle of each moment.

This love our children bring,
fills us so completely
that we are never the same.
But what do we really
give our children?

Deep down we learn
we give them
only one lasting gift.

This gift can never be
exchanged,
or outgrown,
or forgotten.

It is carefully opened
within our child's heart.
It is the gift of ourselves.

We may tell our children how to live...
but what matters to them
is how we live.

They will know
without listening to us
how we feel
about life,
about people,
about nature,
about God.

If we are positive people,
they will be positive too.
If we are helpful
and considerate of others,
they will become helpful
and considerate.

Our children will not always
return to us the kindness
and thoughtfulness we give them.
(Because they are working on
being separate from us.)
But we will see them
being kind and thoughtful to others.

Parents don't always give
the best gift of themselves.
If we are honest, and apologize
for our wrong doing,
we teach our children the value
of forgiving ourselves and others.

We cannot give our children
their deepest emotions, feelings,
and personal experiences.

But we can give them the means
to express who they are,
and how they feel
through art and writing,
poetry and music.

We can show them how
to challenge themselves
and others
through games and sports.

They will come to know
their own uniqueness
as they give expression
to their own experiences.

We will come to know
their own uniqueness
when we watch
and listen to them.

They will flourish
from their successes
and learn from
their mistakes.

There is nothing
harder for parents to bear
than our children's
disappointments
hurtful times, and pain.

There is nothing
more wonderful to share
than our children's joy.

In time, our children
will become completely
who they are.
They will give to others
the gift of their own unique self.

The years of childhood will fade,
and the time we have had
with our children will seem so short.
But what will be remembered
as the one gift that mattered most
to our children...
is the gift we gave of ourselves.

Transformation

We go back through the park
on our way to the Post Office
and my daughter begs to play.

And I watch her
as I remember all the times we came here
when she was one, two, and three.
And I had to watch her every moment and help,
and wipe sand off her bottom,
and tears from her eyes when she fell.

Now she is six and confident,
capable, and coordinated.

And I watch as she spins the merry-go-round.

But as I stand here
I have this eerie feeling about myself...
about the way I was
when I used to come to the park,
about the way I viewed the world,
the way I viewed my life.

I feel so unlike the other person
who used to come to the park.
The other person whose world denied
the existence of conflict, doubt and pain...
whose only tool for problem solving
was never to see problems.

I feel haunted and cold
as drops of rain begin to fall
one by one.

I call to my daughter
knowing we have shared each other's years
of growing up.

Conversation On The Patio

He said
"You know it's hard
to just sit here
when there are things
that could be done."

I stood and listened to my dad,
not wanting to sit
for fear it would change his energy
and he would be silent
once again.

"I don't really like t.v.
And I never really have liked to read.
So what am I supposed to do?"
He looked at me,
and then off into the yard.
"I guess this is all I can do."

He sat in the sun
on a canvas chair
with his legs up
on another chair.

And I kissed him on his lips.
"Dad," I said, "You've had setbacks,
and you've made it through them.
You will become stronger."

"Yes" he said, "I think I will be better this summer."

He didn't know
what a gift
he had given me,
just talking
about himself.

November

I keep it at a distance
but this morning I let it in.

This beautiful morning with the feel of November
when the sun is not warm but bright.
This beautiful morning when my son and husband
leave early for a surfing contest,
when my daughter and her friends
go to the bakery in their pajamas
and chatter about their soccer game
which is today.

This beautiful morning when I come to my office
to finish work on my new book,
work that I feel good about,
work that I love doing...
Scenes of flowers
and memories of beauty...
This morning it is here with me.

It is the song of sorrow
I sing with my parents who are suffering.
Dad with his heart surgery
and Mom with her depression.
It fills me in my heart
and rolls out as tears
through my nose and eyes.
It makes me remember
that I am a part of it all,

the beauty of the morning
the joy of what the day will bring
and the sadness I hold inside.

I hold this sadness today,
the distance is gone.
I am full.

Letter to Mother   Summer 1978

Mother,

I always cry when I say good-bye to you. It's not from
sadness but from all the love you always give and I
always feel. When I return home, I know you have been
here. The garden looks cared for, the house is neat and
clean, we have more ironed clothes in the closet, the
freezer holds homemade soup for a future dinner. But
even more than these things that you always seem to
accomplish in a happy and effortless way, while being a
loving Grandma and playing with Brent— you leave me
with a feeling for my higher values in life. You rekindle
my basic belief that goodness and giving and loving
bring a life of sweetness and joy. But these virtues come
from a free and happy spirit which you possess. They
cannot come from discipline and self-denial. Goodness
and giving and loving in their purest sense come from
within. You do not think "I'll be good to him or I will
give him love." You just feel and live these virtues.
Being around you makes me happy. I feel akin to your
spirit, and so when you leave...I have tears in my eyes.

A young friend of our family was in a drug rehabilitation program. I wanted to write her a letter, but didn't know what to say. I was sitting in my office and looking at a poster above my desk. The museum print was of art from ancient India. It was a simple design, showing three flowers on a faded gold fabric background. What struck me was that the middle flower was tall and full of itself, dwarfing the flowers on each side. The pink tulip had fulfilled its potential, whereas the blue iris on the right and the red-petaled flower on the left had not yet grown. The pink tulip reminded me of the sublime gift that awaits us when we become our own true selves. This I could write to our friend.

The painting speaks to all of us, to help us remember that we can fulfill our own potential. Like flowers, we need time, and light, and nurturing to grow and blossom. We can stay connected to our own inner lives. We can take time for ourselves by writing in a journal, praying, meditating, or taking solitary walks. We can find in those special moments that we are in the company of someone extraordinary... our own true self. S.F.

Gifts of
Your Self

Be All That You Are

Be all that you are.
The sun will find you,
give you her warmth,
and bless you
with her golden touch
as you awaken.

The wind will call you
as you gently bend
and become open
to the world
that surrounds you.

The soil will ground you.
The water will nourish you.
You have been planted here.
The world is yours,
to enjoy, to expand,
to go wherever you want.

Life is the gift
you have been given.
Love is the blessing you can feel.
It is all around...
in the flowers...
in the trees...
in the meadows...
on the mountaintops.

Give yourself a chance.
Give yourself some time,
to know who you are
to become all that you already are.

Accept the gifts of the new day.
Be a part of every person
who says hello.

We are all just hearts
alone and together.
Beating to the music inside,
fulfilling our ambitions,
finding our places
in the wonder of the universe.

More than to hope in yourself,
may you believe in yourself.

Take your own hand
on your own journey.
In the quiet you will hear
the voice of wisdom.
In the stillness you will realize
your deepest dreams
and in your heart
you will know how deeply
you are loved.

Time Alone

Today I know a little more about
who I am...
because I realize who I am not.

Every day I see myself
in a new way...
and this is okay.

Sometimes the hardest thing
I must force myself to do,
is not to do.

The most important discovery
I make day by day
is realizing
what is real
and what is not real...
for me.

I am here
breathing my own portion of air,
seeing images,
hearing, feeling, touching, tasting,
experiencing the world
in my own unique way.

On Being Happy

I once wrote a song
that no one sang.
I once wrote a poem
that no one read.
I once painted a picture
that no one saw.

and I wondered...
why did I do these things?

Then one day
I sang my song
and I read my poem
and I saw my picture...

and I knew why
and I was happy.

Your Journey

There is a journey awaiting you.
It comes in truth and promise,
when you reach the point
of not knowing who you are,
or where to go.

This most precious
but painful passage
is the journey to yourself.

You will travel to places
never before visited,
where you meet unspoken fears,
and unearth buried truths.

You will climb high
and perilous mountains,
those that rise up
from inside yourself.

You will explore
forgotten waters
held deep in the sea of your soul.

You will be stranded in the wilderness
and find a way through pathless land.

You will be lost
before you are found.
You will be empty
before you are full.

You will cry
the deep sobs of the earth.
Tears of rain
will cleanse the house
around your heart.

In time,
because life
like birth and death
knows its own time,
your fears and struggles
and unknowing
will be transformed.

You will become a mountain place
where eagles soar.

You will become a reflecting pool
which sees and knows
the mysteries of your life.

Your heart will be light like a butterfly
as you follow the currents of its true desires.
The flight of the honeybee will be yours,
as you seek the nectar
of what brings sweetness to your daily life.

Most of all you will become who you truly are.
Your heart will hold truth and promise and meaning.
And the heart of the heavens will hold your heart.

More Time Alone

The only dreams I can make come true
are the dreams I have for myself.
The dreams I have for other people
will come true only if they belong to them.

Before I can live successfully
with another person,
I have to be able to live successfully
with myself.

Some of my most crowded moments
are when I am alone.

Sometimes I feel
I am moving through life.
Sometimes I feel
life is moving through me.

There are two things I have learned.
Nothing is for sure.
Life does not get easier.

God may not answer your problems.
But you will answer them.
That is God within you.

I hold my life dear...
like a newborn baby.

Go To Meet the Sadness

Go to meet the sadness.
Go to where the deepest feelings lie.

Go to the bottom, it's okay.
They won't hurt you.
Hold them, have them.
They are a part of you...
just as the rising sun
and the full moon
and the owl on the telephone wire
hooting in the dark are part of you...
They are yours.
Sadness is yours.
Joy will be yours too.
It is all you...and you are all of it.

Having Hope

Hope is seen in the eyes.
Hope is heard in the voice.
Hope is held in the heart.

Hope is alive...it is all around us.
Hope is in the oak tree within the acorn.
Hope is the winged butterfly within the cocoon.
Hope is the first rosebud of Spring
awakening in the stem of Winter's rose.

Hope is not blind.
Hope sees beyond to what it is.
Hope sees through the clouds to the mountain tops,
and journeys over high peaks,
knowing that on the other side
a green valley awaits.

Hope is invisible...
yet it can be seen
when the eyes are closed.

Hope sees the real light of the sun
as it shines within...
and the real power of love
as it fills the heart.

Hope sees beyond our differences to oneness...
and beyond our appearances to the heart.

Hope knows goodness lives
everywhere in this world,
and miracles are happening everyday.

Hope lives with acceptance of the unknowing everyday.

Hope does not ask when the darkness will end
but wonders when the light will begin.

Hope is a way of seeing...
a way of believing...
a way of knowing.

Hope is alive
Hope is here.
Hope is real.

Peaceful Feelings

I sit on the deck
and watch the purple Jacaranda
color this evening's stillness
as one cricket performs solo.

The ruby roses
peek over the swordfern
and Jim tries to catch Mazy,
Emily's little white kitty,
and bring her in for the night.

Distant music from town
filters up Foothill Road,
and a dog barks far away.
It is a peaceful evening in Ojai.
I am peaceful.

In the fall of 1988 I made a journey with my cousin Linda to visit her Dad, whom I called Uncle Pop. He was special to me. Pop had been diagnosed with Alzheimer's Disease and knowing how this illness progresses, I wanted to be able to see him, and in my own way, say good-bye.

It was wonderful to return to the ranch where my Aunt and Uncle lived and where I had spent long summer weeks. My cousin and I had as our childhood playground the pastures, and barns, the stream and slimy-bottomed reservoir. We drank iced tea from fresh well water and ate vine-ripened tomato sandwiches. I remember my Uncle Pop in his jeans and cowboy boots, his smiling twinkling eyes, and balding head beneath the cowboy hat. But Uncle Pop wasn't really there when I arrived. He was well on his way to the place where only those with his illness dwell. He didn't know me or his daughter. He barely knew his wife. But he remembered his mother and told stories of his childhood. He would say to Aunt Annie, "Come here and watch the sun coming through the window." That night when I returned to my home, I sat in the living room and wrote my feelings about time, and that all we have is right now.

"Now is the time," I wrote, "to say I love you to the ones we love."

S.F.

Gifts
of Loving

S.F.

The Gift of Time

Now is the time to stop and watch the sun's rays
as they sparkle through the windows of our lives.

Now is the time to say "I love you"
to the ones we love.

Now is the time to listen to each other.

Now is the time to talk about our deepest desires,
to hold hands with each other's dreams,
to share the joy and the sadness held within.

Now is the time to put aside the chatter of small things,
and to know that time is all we have.

Now is the time to celebrate the small joys of this day,
to notice the light and shadows.

It may be time to dance,
It may be time to grieve,
It may be time to remember,
It may be time to regret.

It may be time to forgive,
It may be time to forget.

Yesterday is always with us,
yet yesterday is always gone.

Tomorrow rides on the horizon
like a bird on the wing.
Tomorrow is a flower opening,
a butterfly emerging from its cocoon.

Today is fullness like a fruit when it is ripe,
like a benevolent rose,
fully opened, to the sun, to the rain,
giving of itself entirely.

Today can nourish and inspire us like no other time.

Treasure the moments of the new dawn,
of the dew on the lawn,
of the sun's journey through the sky.

And after the crimson light has fallen,
when only the lavender hue of first night remains,
as the stars begin their ritual twinkle,
let our hearts touch and be full of thanks,
this gift of time is all we have.

For People in Love

May you stay in the heart of love,
where caring, passion and understanding
become a way of living with each other
and all people.

May you stay in the heart of love,
where all things become possible and beautiful,
where you can see the wonder
and hear the music of the day.

May love call you to its side and whisper its message,
that caring deeply for another enriches your life
and changes the way you see the world.

This wonderful feeling of connection
will help you relate to people everywhere.

May love teach you to speak the language of the heart.

Together you can learn
how important are those things
that enliven and enrich each of you.

Together you can listen to each other's dreams.

Together you can bring to your lives
an understanding of your differences.

You will know that you are each responsible
for your own happiness.

May love be gentle enough
to change with you,
and strong enough to hold you together
when life questions love.

For it is in those difficult times
when problems arise
that you each have the greatest opportunity to grow.

Because you love each other
you can look within your heart,
and see the hurt,
and stay with the unknowing.

Because you love each other
you can be transformed.
Because you love each other
you will find new meaning in life
and its mysterious ways.

The lessons learned from loving each other
will make you more whole,
more real people.

The lessons learned from loving each other
are gifts to help you discover yourself.

May all the days of your lives
be blessed with the joy and the truth
of living fully in the heart of love.

What Love Is

Love is like a stream running free
It is moving, flowing, letting go.

Love is the freedom of water
running over and around
rocks and boulders.

Water cannot easily move boulders.
It learns to go around obstacles
creating ripples, waterfalls,
energy, and momentum.

Sometimes rocks and boulders
build up and block love in our lifestream.

There is love in our lives
wanting to run free.
There are hidden pools...
love stored deep in our hearts.

To get love flowing
I have to see what is blocking it.

Hurt feelings, insecurities,
jealousy, anger, and fear
are rocks and boulders.

It is hard to move boulders.
It is easier to learn how to live with them
how to go around them,
how to get past them.

Admitting to myself that I am hurt,
insecure, jealous, angry, or afraid;
is difficult, painful, humbling...
and sometimes impossible.

But when I understand
that having these feelings
is a part of being human,
when I can accept
and forgive myself
then love can begin to flow.

The flow of love
will gently change
our hurt, and anger, and fear...
into understanding,
inner strength, and acceptance.

As we begin to move through life
like the waters of a stream
the obstacles in our way
will bring new meaning.

They will challenge us
to look at ourselves and
understand ourselves.
They can change our life stream.

Like water carving rock canyons
and creating verdant valleys,
the power of love can shape us.

Love is the stream running free,
inside the heart of you
inside the heart of me.

When You Lose Someone You Love

When someone you love dies
a part of yourself dies too.

For as much as the one you loved
did not belong to you,
your heart belonged to them.
You were a part of each other.

There is a physical hurt within you.
It is as real as the emptiness
that surrounds you.

You will wonder how you will walk
in a world that no longer holds
the footprints of your loved one.

You will wonder how the world can go on
when your world has stopped.

You will speak silently
in the language of tears,
as your heart seeks to understand
what it cannot.

Spiritual thoughts, religious beliefs
and philosophy
may not take away the hurt.

But the power of love will comfort you.

Love will be found in the hearts
of those who surround you and care about you.

People who have been in the place of sadness
where you are now,
will be there for you.

The sun will continue to rise,
and the moon and the stars
will still light the heavens.
You will begin the sacred daily ritual
of "remembering."

Your grief will become your traveling companion,
the part of you that is compassionate, strong, and deep.

In your suffering you will be given
the greatest challenge you will ever have,
to be able to accept what life gives,
and what life takes away.

Peace will come to your days
as you begin to live again
accepting the mysteries
that are a part of life.

With time, the veil of sorrow will lift,
and you will see what is most precious
and most sacred is the love we share
with the ones we love.

Peace will come to your heart
and you will know this love
is an eternal gift.

This love lives forever.

We gathered together for a weekend in the Santa Cruz mountains. After 20 years. Six high school friends. Forget-Me-Nots grew wild and their blue blossoms greeted us as we walked up the path of softened redwood needles to the cabin. Like gifts for the altar of our memories, we had brought flowers, music, bread, and wine. Sitting around the dancing firelight, our conversation sparked with abundant honesty. We talked of difficult times and painful passages. In the truth of sharing, we empowered each other with the gift of our own humanity. We gave each other courage to accept our lives, and in accepting, courage to move on. We walked on the beach, our conversations never beginning and never ending. We were friends. The twenty years apart did not matter. And now we meet once a year and celebrate the gifts of our friendship.

Friends give each other a safe dwelling place where their lives can be shared. In the heart of friendship giving and receiving truly become one.   S.F.

The Gifts of Friends

A Simple Place

We are all a part of each other.
I know no more than this.

I am you.
And you are me.

Because the more I know myself,
The more I know you.

And the more you become,
The more I become.

Life is a place where I am living and dying and dancing.
Life is a place where I am becoming.
And I go on
because I hear the music
and I try to listen, learn, and grow.

Friendship is a Special Place

Friendship is a special place
untouched by time or distance,
where feelings are felt
and thoughts are shared
with someone special.

Friendship gives
to heart and soul
a voice that is heard
in complete trust and understanding.

True friends come into our lives
at special times and stay.
We travel separate journeys
and cross different bridges
with each other's help
and the wonderful feeling that we are not alone.

Friends become our chosen family.
The ties are spun with love and care.

Through our friends
We come to know each other's families,
and learn of the different experiences
that affect each other's lives.

Because of this we learn something precious and great.
In our joys and our problems,
in our dreams and our work,
we are all different.

And yet we feel each other's
special place of caring within,
and we know that we are all the same.

The most magical part of friendship
is that I can be who I am,
and you can be who you are,
totally.

Together we can laugh
in the midst of a problem,
and find hope in the midst of despair.

By just being ourselves,
we help each other.

You can always return to a friend
and find the same warm feeling.
Whether we are together or far apart
friendship will hold us in its heart.

Friendship is a special place.

I'm glad we're there.

With Friends

If there is one ingredient
which adds warmth and love to our lives
it is friendship.

If there is one relationship
to help us through all of the others,
it is friendship.

Friends surround us
with the beauty of their caring.

With friends we can share
what we see, what we feel,
what we love.

Friends help us with our problems because they listen.
And as they listen we begin to hear
the language of our own hearts.

With friends we can walk along
the remembered paths of our lives
and completely share our experiences.

With friends we can work the soil of forgotten dreams,
that need to be tended, and nurtured once again.
With friends we can plant the seeds
of our heart's new dreams.

We can always return to a friend
like going back to a special place,
and find the same warm feeling
unchanged by time or distance.

Life gives us friends so we can share
the precious times and memorable moments
of being children, and teenagers,
and adults, and parents, and grandparents.

Life gives us friends
so we can share the growing up
and the growing old.

With friends we have a place to go
to be accepted and understood.

Together we can laugh,
together we can cry,
our thoughts are heard,
our feelings are held in the heart of a friend.

With friends our lives are more full,
more rich, more open, beautiful, and blessed.

For A Friend

If I could give you
something
to make you feel better...

I would give you
music
not that you hear
but that you feel
in your heart...
music to move your spirit into lightness.

I would read you a poem
written many years ago
by a deep and thoughtful poet.
so you will not feel alone in your pain.

And I would wish you time alone
in the garden
to feel a part of all that is growing and beautiful.

Connecting

It is not the words
that are spoken
that touch the heart.

It is the connection
that has been made
from heart to heart
because of the words.

This is heart talk.

Kind Words

Kind words
come from kind thoughts.

Kind thoughts
come from a loving heart.

A loving heart
comes from an understanding soul.

An understanding soul
comes from God within.

It is good to have kind thoughts
about someone else.

It is even better to tell them.

There are moments that change me. Sometimes it is only a slight shift in awareness. Other times I know I am "seeing differently." Always in these experiences of awakening, I feel a part of another reality...the spiritual part of life. I think of these as sacred moments.

During an insecure troubling time in my life, I went on a wilderness trip into the Sierra Nevada Mountains. Like a child getting over being afraid of the dark, I wanted to meet my fears and become stronger. Late one afternoon, I was led to an area of massive granite rocks, where I was left alone for three days. I surveyed my "place" and found a patch of dirt on which to pitch a small tent. I had a debilitating altitude headache and was overwhelmed with sadness. I wondered why I felt I had to go so far away from everything to get close to myself. I was alone and scared.

As the sun began its descent through the red ochre sky, I sat on my perch of rocks awaiting the inevitable darkness. I watched the twilight sky transform into soft lavender and the treescape surrounding me blacken. As I waited, imperceptible specks of pulsating light appeared. One by one each evening star revealed itself. The sky slowly deepened into the darkest blue pool, and from its depths infinite stars emerged. Darkness was not coming. The night was dawning. I could see clearly. The heavens were awakening and danced with a million lights.

I felt comforted. I realized that in difficult and dark times there is always light, only it is different. Sacred moments bring us this light by which we can see things differently. S.F.

Gifts of
Sacred
Moments

Taking the Bus to Manhattan

I was apprehensive
about making my way
in the city alone
at night
to an unfamiliar area.

I waited outside
the airline terminal
for the Carey Bus.

I felt sweaty and tense
standing in the dark.

The bus arrived.
I chose to carry on my bags
instead of having them thrown
on top of the others.

I felt like an elephant
boarding with all my bags.
The aisle was so narrow
I bumped and apologized as I moved to the back.

I spotted an empty seat
in the back, on the aisle,
and felt relieved,
until I noticed
the very refined,
almost distinguished,
diminutive man
dressed in a dark suit
occupying the window seat.

I had no choice
but to plop down next to him
with no place for my bags
except my lap.

I casually turned
and smiled
and my reflection in the window
came back at me,
so incredibly disheveled,
next to this meticulous and tranquil gentleman.

I shifted
from the embarrassment of my entry
to the anxiety
of where to get off.

I asked this man next to me
about the scheduled stops
because he looked like he would know.

He asked me at which hotel
I would be staying
and when I replied he said,
"Ah yes, I took a course there once,"
and that he had learned
about his feelings,
and when he was blocking them and suppressing them,
"Like I am doing now," he said.

I wondered what he meant
but said nothing.
I looked over at him
and in the bright bus lights
saw my reflection in the window,
and the black cityscape behind me.

He said to me,
"I have just said good-bye to my wife.
She wanted to return to England
to be buried."

And he was sitting there
with his dark suit
and his hat
and his sorrow
and his respect.
I looked at him and listened.

He said her son had come
to accompany the body
back to her homeland.

He was grateful for that.

He said that she had been sick
for a long time,
and sometimes had resented her being sick
and he had yelled at her.
I said I understood.

He had tears in his eyes
and I had tears in my eyes.
and then we talked honestly
as the city traffic and streets moved by.

He said he planned a trip to Texas
to visit his daughter and enjoy the grandchildren
he had never met.

His stop was coming so he prepared to leave.

(No hugs or handshakes from this stranger
who had shared his soul.)

He walked down the aisle
in precision
with decorum
and descended the stairs into the street.

I watched him
walk into the night...
such a respectable person
returning to his apartment
that would never be the same place again.

I can't describe exactly how I felt
but mostly I felt blessed
to have been chosen.
He had handed me the chalice of his sorrow
and I drank.
He had passed me the pipe of his remorse
and I smoked.

We had partaken in an ancient ceremony,
sacred and solemn,
held in truth and trust.

It did not matter that we were not in a church,
a temple, or a Kiva.
It did not matter that we were strangers
in the back of a bus
moving through New York City
in the night.

While Walking to the Post Office

I walk in the dampness and dullness of the day.
The sky is low and gray
and touches the empty street.

As I walk towards the Post Office
the tower bells begin to ring.
And in the quiet and still of noontime
they ring inside of me.

As each one sounds,
it vibrates through me.
I see myself atop a mountain
in the Himalayas, chanting with each sound
which continues its passage into the distance
of sound becoming no sound.

And I look over to the park
where no one plays.
And I remember when I used to bring
my children and push them on the swings.
I know those times are gone.

And I am sad,
because life is a process of times here and times gone.
I know that life is taking me toward myself,
like being on a mountaintop chanting.
It is the spirit always calling from deep inside.

We are stripped of times and things held dear.
It is this constant chipping away
that makes us smooth.

Classical Music

I always hear beautiful music on the radio
as I drive to work each morning.

Today it was Chinese music with flutes.
I heard every note and the music was in me.

But I wonder is it the music,
or is it the early morning,
when the streets are empty
and the new day rests behind a curtain of fog.
Yes, it is the music in the early morning.

But I wonder again
is it the music,
or is it me
in the early morning
when my mind is clear
and my heart is open.
When I am able to listen completely
to the beauty of the music.

Yes, it is the music,
in the morning,
and it is me
in the music
in the morning.

Old St. Thomas Aquinas Church

We were twenty minutes late for Christmas mass
in the beautiful old church
in downtown Palo Alto.

Mary and I hurried up the concrete steps
to the church where we grew up,
where our brother, David, was an altar boy,
where we sang in the choir loft,
where we giggled so much we couldn't stop,
where I fainted many times
because the incense was so strong
and my father carried me out,
where I said my young confession
so loudly my mother said all could hear,
where the wood was so old it creaked
and the echo of heels and soles turned heads,
where celestial light filtered in
through stained glass windows
manifesting the miraculous.

It was here to this well-loved church
that my sister and I now came,
and as we ascended the steps
a small white-haired woman emerged.
She walked towards us and clutched her breast.
We hurried to help her and she gave us
her son's phone number.

While my sister called her son,
I found the pill for her heart in her purse
and put it under her tongue.
We sat on the cold concrete steps
She put her head on my chest
and I held her like a child.
She was fragile, angelic and soft.

My sister returned, the son arrived.
We went into church--yes late--
and perfectly on time.

At the Village Bakery

She gives me a genuine,
"How are you doing today Susan,"
and reaches for my old-fashioned donut.

"How is your husband," I ask in turn.

With her own special gusto
she looks me in the eye and says,
"He's doing okay,
because I make him do things for himself.
But he doesn't know me.
He talks about Louise but he doesn't know it's me.
Today is our wedding anniversary.
We've been married for forty eight years,"
she says as she counts out my change.

To me this is unbearable sadness.
To Louise this is life.
She smiles as she waits on the next customer,
moving on,
living the Zen I study.

While Driving Through Town

We are already one.
One people.
One tribe.
One nation.

I knew this
without doubt
the day I turned left at Cuyama Street
and drove by the old Ojai cemetery
and looked.

I knew it because at that moment
I realized I breathe
and you breathe
and all people who are living breathe.

The ones who rest beneath the tombstones
do not breathe.

But they did.

They had their days,
their years,
their time,
their chance,
in the here and now.
Today I have mine.

Getting Coffee to Go at the Herb Garden Cafe

They sat at the outdoor table
under the sweet smelling jasmine
and purple wisteria blossoms.

He was hunched over
having finished his lunch
from his wheelchair.

She was still beautiful
in her old age.
She had a puppy at her feet
who was young and strong and full of vitality.

As I passed by
he looked at her deeply
through his thick glasses
and romantically, lovingly,
patted her arm.

I had tears in my eyes
thinking of the courage
it takes to grow old.
Losing eyesight, agility, strength,
needing help to get around.

But I saw in his love for her
there is one thing that never grows old,
but only grows stronger.

This is the heart's ability to love.

After Grocery Shopping

I got a dose of the moon
as I walked out of Bayless Market
at 4:50 p.m.
the time of the sky show
when the Topa Topa mountains
turn metallic plum red
and the clouds
reflect the ochre
of the sun setting in the west.

I got a dose of the moon enormous
as it rested,
effortlessly,
luminous,
above the Topa Topas
and below the clouds.

I got a jolt
and I knew why I existed.
To see the moon,
at that moment,
in that instant,
in Ojai.

I was completely fulfilled
and I knew the Earth is a sacred place.

Ojai Morning

I drive down the hill
and look over at the valley,
extraordinarily green and clear,
and up at the mountaintops
elegantly dusted with snow
on this morning of nature sublime.

I can only think
of the luck I have
to live here
where everyday I enjoy
nature's beauty.

I park on Signal Street
and walk toward the coffee house.
She is coming my way,
an old woman in brown,
using a cane.
She stops me
and touches my arm.
I had never seen her before.
"Have you ever seen the mountains?" she asks.
"Yes," I replied and I told her
what I had just been thinking.
"Sometimes," she said, "I think I live in heaven."
I smiled and looked into her eyes.

We went our opposite ways,
her pace a little slower than mine,
but our vision the same.

Book Design by
Susan Crane Dallas
Editor:
Marilyn Moore
Type set in
Marydale,
Rotis Semi Serif,
Rotis Serif Italic
S.F.